Reflections on the Path to Wholeness
Volume 2

Being
Wonderfully
Made

BRENDA S. JACKSON, PH.D.

*Priority*ONE
publications
Detroit, Michigan, USA

Reflections on the Path to Wholeness: Being Wonderfully Made
Copyright © 2008 Brenda S. Jackson, Ph.D.

All scripture quotations, unless otherwise indicated, taken from the HOLY BIBLE, NEW INTERNATIONAL VERSION®. NIV®. Copyright© 1973, 1978, 1984 by International Bible Society. Used by permission of Zondervan. All rights reserved.

Scripture quotations marked (KJV) are taken from the HOLY BIBLE, KING JAMES VERSION (Authorized).

All poetry submissions herein are © 2000 – 2008 Brenda S. Jackson

All rights reserved. No part of this publication may be reproduced, stored in a retrieval system, or transmitted in any form or by any means – electronic, mechanical, photocopy, recording, or any other – except for brief quotations in printed reviews, without the prior permission of the publisher.

*Priority*ONE Publications
P. O. Box 725 • Farmington, MI 48332
(800) 331-8841 Nationwide Toll Free
E-mail: info@p1pubs.com
URL: http://www.p1pubs.com

ISBN 13: 978-1-933972-09-2

Edited by Patricia A. Hicks
Cover and interior design by PriorityONE Publications

Printed in the United States of America

TABLE OF CONTENTS

Dedication and Acknowledgements 6

Foreword   Elder Michael A. Dixon 7

Introduction   Chaplain Carron M. Caldwell 8

Seminar #1   Who Am I Sexually? 9

Seminar #2   Knowing Who I Am 25

Seminar #3   Victim Mentality 43

Seminar #4   Sheep or Goat 54

Seminar #5   Valuing Diversity 62

Seminar #6   Going Into Leadership 81

About the Author 102

DEDICATION AND ACKNOWLEDGMENTS

For I know the plans I have for you, declares the Lord, plans to prosper you and not to harm you, plans to give you hope and a future. Then you will call upon me and come and pray to me, and I will listen to you. You will seek me and find me when you seek me with all your heart. I will be found by you," declares the Lord, and will bring you back from captivity. I will gather you from all the nations and places where I have banished you, declares the Lord, and bring you back to the place from which I carried you into exile." Jeremiah 29:11-14 NIV

Volume II, "Reflections On The Path To Wholeness, *Being Wonderfully Made*, is dedicated to my Lord and Savior, Jesus, The Christ and with the expectation He will be glorified by all who use the seminars of this book.

It is dedicated to the Simuel Family, especially my son, Derrick Anthony Herbert, and in memory of members who have left this physical world and are rejoicing in Spirit with The Lord: My parents, Lucy and Willie Simuel, my brother, Tyrone Simuel, my sisters, Cleopha Byrd and Willie Lou Jones, my Aunt Nola Settles, and my sister-in law, Mary J. Simuel.

It is dedicated to the churches at Camp Valley Correctional Facility, Huron Valley Women's Correctional Facility, Robert C. Scott Women's Correctional Facility, Ryan Regional Correctional Facility and St. Louis Correctional Facility. I also dedicate this book to the Correctional Facilities of Cape Town, and Pretoria, South Africa where the Lord has opened doors to ministry.

I thank all the Spiritual Leaders assisting in ministry to the incarcerated through BSJ Christian Seminars: Elder Arnoldine Lancaster, Ministers: Ernestine Smith, Lawrence Phillips, Donnie Benion, Jerry Jones-Davis, Deacon Charle Traylor, Brother Peter Clements and sisters: Brenda Rudolph and Mary Johnson.

I thank the members of the Prison Ministry of New Prospect Missionary Baptist Church, especially the Rev. Ron Copeland, and my Pastor, The Rev. Dr. Wilma R. Johnson.

I acknowledge the servants, correctional officers, and Chaplains who facilitated our visiting Jesus in Prison. It is with joy that $2.00 from the sale of each book will be given to the prison ministries of Africa where I have been blessed to serve.

In all things, TO GOD BE THE GLORY!

FOREWORD

The Bible says knowledge is important. As we get knowledge, in all our getting we must also get understanding. If we're going to utilize the knowledge we now have and will receive throughout our lives, understanding is vital. Proverbs 1:7 says that the fear of the Lord is the beginning of knowledge. In other words, true knowledge is a healthy respect for God and His view of life's design and existence, revealed in His Word. This is the core of what it means to have real knowledge and understanding. After all, God knows what makes us tick and what causes us to tock, what can be fixed and what must stop.

Knowledge and understanding work together to enrich and enlighten our journey. I believe the outlines contained in *Being Wonderfully Made* are a godsend that will help us to acquire more of the knowledge and understanding needed to keep us from perishing. It is also written that people are and will continue to perish for lack of knowledge, more specifically, knowledge of the Holy One – God.

With that said, the step-by-step outlines of this book are sure to help make clear distinctions between our thoughts and fact. As I read the outlines written in this book I experienced a burst of excitement and satisfaction of heart and mind as my understanding in these areas increased. I found its contents kept me engaged as I considered the various applications for which I could use each seminar. Like honey following after salt, together they have a flavorful impact. The subjects presented in this text hold much promise for the branches of Christ who long to bear much fruit (John 15:1-2).

The apostle Paul said that we must work out our own salvation with fear and trembling. This work systematically assists with the Kingdom work we must do. The ISO System is a system designed by the British to assist manufacturers in maintaining exceptional standards consistently. For those who would use these outlines to provide biblically sound knowledge and understanding about what it means to be *Wonderfully Made* creations of God, I believe these outlines will be sought after by pastors, chaplains and lay leaders alike to establish and provide training materials that help believers to consistently maintain exceptional standards in their walk with God.

Elder Michael A. Dixon

INTRODUCTION

Our world covers people from all walks of life, who seek meanings to their path of wholeness. Minister Dr. Brenda Jackson path of wholeness has launch her into the deep to pursue her calling in facilitating seminars behind the walls of incarnated prisoners. Some of the seminars speak of unadulterated topics and interpretation that is a *hush* in some of our pulpits.

In Minister Dr. Jackson's first Volume *A Journey of Redeeming Faith,* she facilitates the journey in being able to see the beam in one's own eye, with not always focusing on the mote in another's eye. The journey of this volume takes the path of wholeness of ownership, with the grace of God along the way. For Volume 2 *Being Wonderful Made* echoes the power of scriptures from a theological and educational base, which reaches mankind from all levels to facilitate God's word in seminars.

Each seminar topic of scripture looms to what God says about his path of truth:

- There was homosexuality, an abomination for mankind to lie with the same sex
- There was sexual relationships, made in the image of God
- Lot was called out, "Bring out the two men."
- Victim, in the web of one's past
- Victory, in newness of life in Christ Jesus
- We have biblical leaders, who followed the plan of God
- Here I am individually, knowing oneself holistically
- Here comes collectively, knowing others through relationships

As the seminars are being facilitated, they bring out the talents and gifts as many prisoners realized how they allowed Satan to use their gifts and talents for ungodly things. Volume 2 pulls out biblical leaders that God used to fall under his leadership. This volume also brings the students to the seminars as participants to discuss and write their answers and beliefs to some challenges and thought provoking subjects.

As Minister Dr. Jackson travels behind the walls to facilitate seminars, she volunteers countless hours to collaborate the meaning of scriptures in seminars. The seminars are based on biblical principals that are interwoven in one's path of wholeness.

Chaplain Carron Marie Caldwell. B.S., Th.B.

Chapter 1
WHO AM I SEXUALLY?

Sexual Orientation
&
Sexual Lifestyle

BSJ Christian Seminars
Minister Brenda Simuel Jackson, Ph.D.
© 2007 All rights reserved.

Reflections on Who Am I?
© 2007 Brenda Simuel Jackson

Who am I? Abstinence is my name, freedom from sin is my game.

Who am I? A Nubian Queen, a Black woman is what I mean.

Who am I? One with an education, recognizing life is not a vacation.

Who am I? A helper to others, to one man child an absent mother.

Who am I? A good neighbor I seek to be,
not a passer by filled with fear is she.

Who am I? A saved sinner filled with The Holy Spirit;
seeking my reward in heaven whenever they are given.

Wonderfully Made
© 2007 Brenda Simuel Jackson

In His likeness, He fashioned me.
My authority of His creation my stewardship I see.

Bones knitted together to do His Will,
A mind like Christ to think and to feel.

My eyes He opened that I may see,
The mysteries of His coming, just for me.

My ears He let hear the wonders of His creation,
and with my tears I offer Him praise and adoration.

The beauty of character with blessings of His strength and His might,
that removes all oppression and fears that come in the night.
How wonderful it is to be made for His light.

SEMINAR OBJECTIVES

- Understand the differences between sexual orientation and homosexual lifestyles

- Understand Biblical truths regarding homosexual lifestyle

- Understand the Biblical perspective of Christian homosexuals

- Understand how the Church is to love the homosexual Christian and witness to the homosexual sinner

- Understand Spiritual issues of same sex marriages

- Learn Scriptural tools for the warfare

I. Act of homosexuality and sexual orientation are separate:
  A. Heterosexual orientation:
     1. Sexual desires directed toward person of opposite sex
     2. Conscious impulse toward opposite sex
     3. Craving for opposite sex
  B. Homosexual orientation:
     1. Desire toward member(s) of one's own sex
     2. Craving for member of one's own sex
  C. Biblical definition:
     1. Homosexuality is behavior
     2. Homosexuality is not desire
     3. Homosexuality is sexual intercourse with person of same sex
  D. Homosexual – one who chooses to engage in sexual activity with person of same sex (Hunt, p.5-8)
  E. Homosexuality is erotic activity with person of same sex:
     1. Lesbian - female homosexual,
     2. Bi-sexual:
        a. sexual behavior involving males, and females,
        b. participates in heterosexual and homosexual relations.
     3. Pervert (αρσενοκστησ):
        a. Male who practices homosexuality
        b. A pederast
        c. A sodomite
        d. One given to some form of sexual perversion
  F. Transsexual - emotional desire to be the opposite sex:
     1. Feels trapped in a body of wrong gender
     2. Undergoes surgery to modify sex organs

G. Transvestite:
   1. Cross dresses
   2. Adopts garments and often characteristic behavior of opposite sex
   3. Achieves emotional or sexual satisfaction
   4. Usually not a homosexual or transsexual

II. Biology of Homosexuality:
A. A person is not born a homosexual according to DNA data. (Ping)

B. Homosexuality is behavior not identity

C. Homosexual behavior may be natural behavior
   1. Homosexual behavior is sin.
   2. Sin is natural for unbeliever.
   3. Cravings may be natural for believer and unbeliever.

III. Kenzie Studies - "Beyond Self-Identification":
A. Scale of sexual orientation 0 to 6:
   1. 0=exclusively heterosexual through post puberty
      a. socio-sexual contacts of opposite sex
      b. responses to opposite sex
   2. 1=incidental homosexual experience:
      a. due to circumstances such as prison or military
      b. physical contact
      c. psychic response
      d. may occur single time
      e. infrequent in comparison to heterosexual experiences
      f. includes never acted on feelings
   3. 2=more than incidental experiences:
      a. definite responses to homosexual stimuli
      b. definite physical response
      c. definite psychological response
   4. 3=is equally homosexual and heterosexual:
      a. mid-way on scale
      b. equally homosexual/heterosexual in overt experiences

  c. equally homosexual/heterosexual in psychic reactions
 5. 4=more homosexual than heterosexual:
  a. have overt homosexual activity and/or psychic reactions
  b. maintains fair amount of heterosexual activity
  c. maintains fair amount of response to heterosexual stimuli
 6. 5=almost entirely homosexual in overt activities or reactions
  a. experience with opposite sex is incidental
  b. sometimes reacts psychically to individuals of opposite sex
 7. 6=exclusively homosexual:
  a. overt homosexual experiences
  b. exclusive psychic reactions

B. Development of sexual feelings (Ping):
 1. Studies of females:
  a. heterosexual/homosexual equally likely to have attraction to opposite gender
  b. females have an even distribution on the Kenzie scale
  c. 1/3 identify in heterosexual range (0-1)
  d. 1/3 identify in bi-sexual range (2-4)
  e. 1/3 identify in homosexual range (5-6)
 2. Studies of males:
  a. early development of sexual feelings directed toward gender they eventually identify as:
   i. males either primarily heterosexual (0-1)
   ii. males either primarily homosexual (5-6)
   iii. bi-sexual range uncommon

IV. Biblical perspective of homosexuality/sexual orientation:
A. Biblically, in literal sense, the Bible deals with homosexual behavior, not homosexual desires

B. Nearly every reference to homosexuality is <u>performance</u> of sex with person or persons of same sex (Richards, 492)

C. Homosexual acts are condemned in both Testaments:
   1. Leviticus 20:13 – *"If a man lies with a man as one lies with a woman, both of them have done what is detestable. They must be put to death."*
   2. Leviticus 18:22 – *"Do not be with a man as one lies with a woman that is detestable."*
   3. Romans 1:26-27 – Paul describes both the behavior of lesbian and homosexual lifestyles:
      a. unnatural
      b. indecent
      c. motivated by shameful lusts
      d. perversion
      e. acts of a depraved mind
   4. 1 Timothy 1:10 – Homosexual behavior is described:
      a. among acts of law breakers/rebels
      b. as equal to adultery

D. Moral character of person shown through behavior:
   1. Read Genesis 19:1-14:
      a. "The two angels arrived at Sodom in the evening, and Lot was sitting in the gateway of the city. When he saw them, he got up to meet them and bowed down with his face to the ground."
      b. "My lords," he said, "please turn aside to your servant's house. You can wash your feet and spend the night and then go on your way early in the morning. 'No,' they answered, 'We will spend the night in the square....' "
      c. "But he insisted so strongly that they did go with him and entered his house. He prepared a meal for them, <u>baking bread without yeast</u> and they ate."
      d. "Before they had gone to bed, all the men from every part of the city of Sodom - both young and old - surrounded the house."

e. "They called to Lot, "Where are the men who came to you tonight? Bring them out to us so that we can have sex with them."

f. "Lot went outside to meet them and shut the door behind him, and said, "No, my <u>friends</u> [Hebrew word is brother , used in the widest sense possible meaning like or kindred], don't do this <u>wicked</u> thing."

g. "Look, I have two daughters [betrothed to men of Sodom, but virgins] who have never slept with a man. Let me bring them out to you, and you can do what you like with them. But don't do anything to these men, for they have come under the protection of my roof."

h. "Get out of our way, "they replied and they said, "This fellow [Lot] came here as an alien, and now he wants to play the judge. We'll treat you worse than them. They kept bringing pressure on Lot and moved forward to break down the door."

i. "But the men inside reached out and pulled Lot back into the house and shut the door."

j. "Then they struck the men who were at the door of the house, young and old, with <u>blindness</u> so they could not find the door."

k. "The two men said to Lot, "Do you have anyone else here - sons-in-law, sons, or daughters, or anyone else in the city who belongs to you? Get them out of here,"

l. "Because we are going to destroy this place. The outcry to the Lord against its people is so great that he has sent us to destroy it."

m. "So Lot went out and spoke to his sons-in-law, who were pledged to marry his daughters. He said, "Hurry and get out of this place, because the Lord is about to destroy the city, "But his sons-in-law thought he was joking."

2. Description of moral character:
   a. describe Lot's moral character and behavior:
      i. hospitable
      ii. ancient hospitality, host obliged to protect the guest
      iii. moral (knows what is wicked)
      iv. had no persuasive power
   b. why Lot would offer his daughters:
      i. protect his guests.
      ii. depicts differences in orientation
      iii. request for natural behavior ignored
3. Compare Judges 19:13 - 20:48:
   a. The Levite and his Concubine:
      i. illustrates spiritual chaos
      ii. 12 tribes united in treaty like organization
      iii. in territory of Benjamin - Gibeah
      iv. men wanted the Levite, took the concubine, raped her repeatedly until she died
      v. concubine, a secondary wife
   b. attitude of men of Gibeah - lust
   c. attitude of men of Gibeah - political power
   d. compare men of Sodom with men of Gibeah
   e. compare Lot to the homeowner
   f. compare Lot to the Levite
   g. compare events
   h. what does this say about homosexual behavior?
4. Canaanite religion promoted homosexual prostitution – I Kings 14:24
   a. there were even male shrine prostitution in the land
   b. the people engaged in all detestable practices of nations the Lord had driven out before the Israelites
   c. emphasis is on behavior
5. Scriptural, homosexual behavior is an immoral lifestyle.

6. Crimes against Morality:
   a. adultery (1 Corinthians 6:9-11)
   b. unnatural sex acts like homosexuality
   c. prostitution
   d. other forms of perverted sex (Nelson Bible Facts, 388)
7. Disagreement in Corinthian Church about role of sex in the Christian lifestyle:
   a. some felt all life was to be enjoyed, all acts including adultery, prostitution, homosexual acts
   b. others thought sex evil and there should be no physical relations
   c. Paul sought to clarify between moral and immoral, 1 Corinthians 6:9
   "Do you not know that the wicked will not inherit the kingdom of God?
   Do not be deceived: Neither the sexually immoral
   nor idolators
   nor adulterers
   nor male prostitutes
   nor homosexual offenders
   nor thieves
   nor the greedy
   nor drunkards
   nor slanders
   nor swindlers
   will inherit the kingdom of God."
8. 1 Corinthians 6:11 - But you were washed:
   "And that is what some of you were
   But you were washed
   you were sanctified
   you were justified in the name of the Lord Jesus Christ
   Therefore, you can be sanctified and justified by the Spirit of God."
9. No homosexual sin puts a person beyond God's grace.

10. Genesis 1:27-28,31: We are in God's image
    God created man in his own image,
    in the image of God, he created him;
    male and female he created them.
    God blessed them and said to them, be fruitful and increase in number
    fill the earth
    Subdue it
    God saw all that He had made, and it was very good.
11. Homosexual behavior entered with sin.
    a. Adultery after the Fall
    b. Prostitution after the Fall
    c. Law governing sexual behavior, Leviticus 18, after the Fall.

V. Christian Homosexuals:
   A. Intimate non-homosexual, same sex relationships:
      1. David and Jonathan (1 Samuel 18:1),
      2. Paul and Timothy (II Timothyothy 1:3-4),
      3. Naomi and Ruth (Ruth 1:16-17).
   B. A true Christian will not continue as a 5-6 on the behavior scale:
      1. Those who truly born from above will not continue in habitual sin.
      2. In time change of behavior will occur or death will occur, (1 John 5:16-20),
      3. In time, desire to please God will supercede desire to please the flesh, although the struggle may continue.
      4. "No one who is born of God will continue to sin as a lifestyle". (Campolo, study of 300)
   C. In America, 1% of males practice homosexuality:
      1. 5% of American males have homosexual orientation.
      2. 4 out of 5 (80%) of homosexuals do not practice physical behavior, homosexual or heterosexual.
      3. 7% of the celibate homosexuals are in the Church.
      4. Very few instances found where orientation has changed.

D. Christian sin, some struggle with homosexuality (Behavior)
   1. God will not reject,
   2. However, must realize, God's Holy Spirit is in the person,
   3. Have the power to refuse to sin,
   4. Actions for the homosexual Christian:
      a. Run from sexual immorality (1 Corinthians 6:18)
      b. Leave former ways of life (Ephesians 4:22)
      c. Form new attitudes (Ephesians 4:23)
      d. Be godly put on the new self
      e. Remember body is a Temple of God (1 Corinthians 6:19)
E. Christian attitude toward Christian homosexuals:
   1. Harbor no judgment (Matthew 7:1)
   2. Have unconditional love and acceptance (Romans 15:7)
   3. Help them to see selves in Christ (John 1:12
   4. Hedge them in with prayer
   5. Hold the person responsible for choice and change (Romans 14:12)

F. Christian attitude toward non-Christian homosexual:
   1. Remember God created all persons, and we cannot curse.
   2. Opportunity for evangelism - sow seeds
   3. Love thy enemy,
   4. Accept behavior is a sin forbidden by God (Romans 1:26-27)
   5. Pray for their salvation.

G. Breaking The Strong Hold:
   1. Accept that homosexual behavior is sin (Romans 1:26-7),
   2. Know that Jesus sets free from sin (Luke 4:18),
   3. Eliminate belief that personal will power is adequate to free (John 15:5),
   4. Become Christ controlled - yielding the body to Christ (Romans 6:11-14)
   5. Depend on God to meet emotional needs (2 Corinthians 12:9),
   6. Open the door to heterosexual relationships or seek celibacy (1 Corinthians 7:5b - 9; 15:33-34)

7. Focus on godly goals (Hebrews 12:1)
   a. Focus on God's love for you (Jeremiah 31:3)
   b. Respect how wonderfully made you are (Psalm 139:14),
   c. Respond to God's call to live holy (1 Thessalonians 4:7),
8. Focus on embracing true identity (Counseling Through The Bible):
   a. See yourself as a loved child of God,
   b. Accept yourself and your gender as God made you,
   c. Choose to be the person God created,
   d. Concentrate on please God,
   e. Study God's Word,
   f. Pray.

VI. Spiritual concerns Regarding Same Sex Marriages
   A. The Bible describes marriage as a union between one man and one woman.
   B. Marriage is not a simple commitment.
   C. Marriage is not a contract.
   D. Marriage is not simply sexual relationships between two consenting adults.
   E. Marriage is a state in which persons would <u>naturally</u> fulfill respective roles as lived out in Biblical times. (Psalm 45:11, 1 Peter 3:4-6)
   F. Genesis 2:18 - "The Lord God said, "It is not good for the man to be alone....I will make a helper suitable for him...
   G. Genesis 2:22 - "Then the Lord God made a woman from the rib He had taken out of the man and He brought her to the man."
   H. Genesis 2:24 - "For this reason a man will leave his father and mother and be united to his wife, and they will become one flesh."
   I. Divine intent - monogamy
   J. Divine intent inseparable union
   K. Marriage symbolizes the union between God and His people. (Nelson):

1. Ephesians 5:23 - For the husband is the head of the wife as Christ is the head of the Church, His body of which He is the Savior.
2. Same sex marriages cannot demonstrate Jesus as head of the Church.
3. 2 Corinthians 11:2 - "I am jealous for you with a godly jealousy. I promised you to one husband, to Christ. So that I might present you as a pure virgin to Him."

L. The Bible describes Jesus - The Bridegroom
   1. The Church, The Bride
   2. The marriage relationship between a man and woman represents our relationship with Jesus

VII. Scriptures to Assist Breaking the Stronghold:

A. 1 Corinthians 6:18: "Flee from sexual immorality. All other sins a man commits are outside his body, but he who sins sexually sins against his own body."

B. 2 Corinthians 5:17: "Therefore, if anyone is in Christ, he is a new creation; the old has gone, the new has come."

C. Luke 1:37: "Nothing is impossible with God."

D. Romans 6:11-12: "In the same way, count yourselves dead to sin but alive to God in Christ Jesus. Therefore do not let sin reign in your mortal body so that you obey its evil desires."

E. 1 Corinthians 6:19-20: "You are not your own; you were bought at a price. therefore honor God with your body."

F. 2 Peter 1:3: "His divine power has given us everything we need for life and godliness through our knowledge of Him who called us by His own glory and goodness."

BIBLIOGRAPHY

Alsop, John R. (ed.) *An Index to the Revised Bauer-Arndt-Gingrich Greek Lexicon.* 2nd Ed. Grand Rapids: Zondervan Publishing House, 1981.

Barker, Kenneth. Gen Ed. *The NIV Study Bible.* Grand Rapids, MI: Zondervan Bible Publishers. 1985.

Bauers, Walter, Gingrich, F. Wilbur, Danker, Frederick W. (Eds.) *A Greek-English Lexicon of the New Testament and Other Early Christian Literature.* 2nd ed. Chicago: Moody Press, 1979.

Campolo, Tony & Peggy, " Is the Homosexual My Neighbor?" A transcript of a Videotape of a Talk at North Park College Chapel on February 29, 1996. Retrieved 12/20/2004 (http://www.bridges-across.org/ba/campolo.htm).

Gower, Ralph. *The New Manners and Customs of Bible Times.* Chicago: Moody Press, 1987.

Hunt, June, "Homosexuality a Case of Mistaken Identity", in *Counseling Through The Bible,* Vol III, 2004, 5-49.

Packer, J.I., Tenney, Merrill C., White Jr., Williams. *Illustrated Encyclopedia of Bible Facts,* Vol 2, Life in Bible Times, HALO Press, 1995.

Ping, M.D, April Joy. Lectures given at Ecumenical Theological Seminary, January 8-12, 2007, Detroit, Michigan, "Medical Science and Theology in Dialogue".

Richards, Ph.D., Lawrence O. *The Revell Bible Dictionary.* New Jersey: Fleming H. Co., 1990.

Vine, W.E. , Unger, Merrill, F. White, Jr., William. *Vines Complete ExpositoryDictionary of Old and New Testament Words.* Nashville: Thomas Nelson Publishers, 1985.

Chapter 2
KNOWING WHO I AM

BSJ Christian Seminars
Minister Brenda Simuel Jackson, Ph.D.
© 2007 All rights reserved.

WHO AM I
© 2007
Brenda Simuel Jackson

Who Am I?
The 9th child of Willie and Lucy Simuel.
Who Am I?
Miss 5 by 5, book worm, not at all beautiful.
Who Am I?
Mother worked afternoons, Daddy worked days, often was he gone.
Sis always tried to lose me, and put me in a maze.
Who Am I?
One loved by Jesus, not going to hell,
Jesus loves me even though I fail.
Who Am I?
One who learned family love in many different ways,
The older I grew, the more love of Jesus and family I knew.
Who Am I?
A fornicator, an adulterer, a taster of weed;
God forgave me, from sin I was freed
Who Am I?
A child of God,
A disciple of Christ,
A daughter to parents who loved me,
A sibling to siblings who care willingly.
Who Am I?
A minister of God's Word,
A minister seeking to make Jesus heard.

SEMINAR OBJECTIVES

Participants will understand and apply the following principles:

- Knowing self is only through relationship

- Knowing self is identifying self-defeating attitudes.

- Knowing self is transforming from a victim to a victor.

OVERVIEW OF SELF AWARENESS PRINCIPLES

LEVEL III

WHO AM I IN RELATION TO OTHERS? Social Systems: Family (Ephesians 5:22-6:4) Work (Ephesians 6:5-9; Romans 13:1-10 Community (Luke 10)
Therefore confess your sins to one another, and pray for one another, so that you may be healed, the effective prayer of a righteous man can accomplish much. James 5:16 NASB

LEVEL II

WHO AM I IN RELATIONSHIP TO ME? Self-Esteem based on a relationship with Christ Building Blocks: Remember who I am in Christ Recognizing God's plan for me Knowing what I can accomplish through Christ Recognizing my potential
Know the inner-self; walk in the Spirit, and overcome the evils of the flesh. Galatians 5:16-26

FOUNDATION LEVEL I

WHO AM I IN RELATION TO GOD? Made in the image and likeness of God Redeemed, justified, and reconciled back to God through Christ Return of God-likeness A Child of The King
"I praise You, because I am fearfully and wonderfully made." Psalms 139:14 NIV

FOUNDATION LEVEL I

A. Who I am in relation to God:
   a. Made in the image and likeness of God
   b. Redeemed, justified, reconciled back to God through Christ
   c. Return of God-likeness
   d. A Child of The King

B. Psalms 139:14 - I will praise you, for I am fearfully and wonderfully made…

C. Genesis 1:26-27 Made in the image and likeness of God.
"Then God said "Let us make man in our image, according to our likeness; let them have dominion over the fish of the sea, over the birds of the air, and over the cattle, over all the earth and every creeping thing that creeps on the earth. So God created man in His own image, in the Image of God He created him; male and female He created them." (New Scofield NKJV)

D. Hebrew word for image:
   a. Representation
   b. Something fashioned
      - lifeless
      - same word used for idol
      - we did not evolve

E. The Hebrew word for likeness means a quality or condition of similarity:
   a. Genesis 2:7: "Then the Lord God formed man of dust from the ground, and breathed into his nostrils the breath of life; man became a living being." (NASV)
      - the original air breathed by man was divine, not created.
      - our likeness is being a living being, "God Is"
      - God's breath in us is eternal, and similar to the eternality of God
      - eternality: Acts 17:28-29: "…for in Him we live, move, and have our being…For we are His offspring."

- b. The divine nature of God in man allowed fellowship with God.
  - Adam and Eve initially enjoyed fellowship
  - sin broke their fellowship
- c. Our likeness is an intellectual ability.
  - man is the highest form of being
  - man named all of the animals
  - read Genesis 2:19-20; 1:28
- d. Our likeness includes ruler-ship – God given authority to rule

F. Christ provided the means for restoration of our Godly likeness:
  - a. Jesus Christ rescued us from the penalty of sin. (John 3:16-17)
  - b. We confess and believe. (Romans 10:8-10)
  - c. We regain righteousness because of our redemption, justification, and reconciliation.
    - our likeness includes eternality.
    - John 17:3
    - Romans 6:23
  - e. Now we have the mind of Christ.
    - regaining righteousness – 2 Corinthians 5:20-21
    - faculty to retain the knowledge given by God
    - understanding God's judgment
    - consciousness of godly counsel
    - ability to obey
    - knowledge of what Christ did for us

G. Jesus changes possibilities into things of substance
  - a. Recognize God's purpose in your life
  - b. Learn to implement God's purposes
  - c. Learn how to push – birth possibilities
  - d. Possibilities come from the word power, able to do.
    - Capacity to produce
    - Being inventive
    - Being resourceful
    - Shaping events

e. Metaphor – The Samaritan Woman at the Well (True Event)
   - Think of your environment as your well
   - Think of your environment as a strategic place for battle
   - Think of your environment as a place to receive the water of life
   - Think of your environment as the place to get spiritually pregnant
   - Testimony from Joseph Williams, *Sheep In Wolves Clothing"*

   "For thirteen years, I lived like a wolf. I lived among the wolves, while avoiding the sheep like a plague. I did as the wolves did, while looking like a wolf, I talked like a wolf. I walked like a wolf. Anyone who saw me assumed I was a wolf. If ever I allowed myself to engage in deep thought for any length of time, I would realize I was not like the other wolves…but I was a lost sheep….Thankfully, I had a Good Shepherd who knew I was lost and would not rest until I was back in the fold. It took a while, but thanks to God's persistence with me, I made it back!…"

ASSESSMENT OF YOUR RELATIONSHIP
(scale adapted from Assessment, Who Am I, Intercristo's Career Kit, 53)

LEVEL I Relationship
__ I thanked God for his workmanship in creating me
__ I have gone where God has sent me
__ I have sought to grow in my understanding of His expectations
__ I confirmed my mission with Him
__ I have accepted responsibility for Gifts/talents invested in me

LEVEL II Relationship
A. Who I am in relationship to me:
   a. self-esteem based on a relationship with Christ.
   b. building blocks:
      - who I am in Christ
      - what I can accomplish through Christ
      - recognizing my potential

B. Galatians 5:16-26:
   a. Know the inner-self
   b. Walk in the Spirit
   c. Overcome the evils of the flesh

C. The New Me – Mirror, Mirror of the Scriptures tell me what I see! (James 1:22-25):
   __ How is your weight of truth?
   __ Are your muscles firm with faith?
   __ Do you see lines of wisdom?
   __ Do you see growth in moral conduct?
   __ Do you see perseverance through trials?
   __ In your humble estate can you see your high status?
   __ Is there any deception in that curl in your hair?
   __ Who won the last battle, flesh or Spirit?
   __ What was your last blessing?

D. Don't be afraid to look in the mirror:

E. We see ourselves through the mirror of someone else.
   a. John's and Joan's perception of self
      __ John's Joan
      __ John's Joan's Joan
      __ Joan's John's Joan
      __ Joan's Joan
      __ John's John's
      __ The real Joan in Christ
   b. Insert your name and the name of a significant other or close friend.
   c. The Tarnished me:
      __ My broken likeness to God
      __ Living by Law and lust of the flesh
      __ Giving in to peer pressure
      __ Giving in to lures of ads and fads
   d. Galatians 5:19-21 (read)

e. Me with a relationship to Christ
   __ Child of the King
   __ Where am I going?
   __ Self-respect, remembering I am in God's likeness.

f. "I will praise You for I am fearfully and wonderfully made." Psalm 139:14 NKJV

g. The Lord has a plan for me. – Psalm 139:16
   "Your eyes saw my substance being yet unformed, and in Your book they all were written. The days fashioned for me when yet there were none of them."

h. New Creature with inner beauty provided by Christ. (Galatians 5:16-26 – Describe Yourself)

i. Recognize your potential:
   - we have a promise like that of God's chosen given at Mt. Gerizim
     - others are to fear you. (Deuteronomy 28:10)
     - you can be the head and not the tail (Deuteronomy 28:13)
       - Promotions
       - Entrepreneurial opportunities
     - you can be above and not beneath (Deuteronomy 28:13)
   - I/you can respect my/yourself:
     - I know who I am
     - I know whose I am
     - I know where I am going

j. Munroe, Myles, *Maximizing Your Potential*:
   - Remember your potential
     - God created you for a special purpose
     - God gave you the potential to fulfill it
     - You are a competent person
     - You must experience a life-changing encounter with Jesus Christ to recover your potential
   - Steps to recover your potential:
     - Accept God's forgiveness
     - See yourself as forgiven

- Move beyond your past
- Use the past as information for the future
- As Christ redeemed you, redeem the remaining days of your life

k. Sometimes we are too busy adding up our troubles; we forget to count the blessings. ("I will remember the works of the Lord; surely I will remember your wonders of old. I will meditate also on all your work, and talk of your doings." Psalm 77:11,12 NKJV)

l. God is in Control – Remember who you are and where you are going!

- Everyone has potential to fulfill God's purpose in their life.

- You cannot maximize your potential if you live in an environment which restricts.

- You cannot maximize your potential if you live in an environment which is not conducive to growth.

- Your potential is lost when you try to live by your own devices.

- Ignorance is a robber.

- "You are valuable and necessary to the destiny of the human race." (Munroe, Dr. Myles, Maximizing Your Potential, 2001. p. 51)

SELF ESTEEM

SCRIPTURES

Psalm 39:13-16
Psalm 119:1,5,6
Matthew 5:3-12
Psalm 119:22
Psalm 32:2
Proverbs 31:18-31

SELF-ESTEEM IS SELF RESPECT

Creation of God
His marvelous work
Blessed of God
No shame
No scorn
No contempt
Obedient to God's statutes
Sins not held against me
No deceit
Seek righteousness
Give mercy
Pure heart
Peacemaker
Industrious
Not lazy
Helper of others
Provides for family
Conducts business with expertise
Has dignity
Has wisdom

Read the Scriptures and select your areas of Self-Esteem which is your basis of self respect.

SELF ASSESSMENT OF LEVEL II RELATIONSHIP

__ What I do is consistent with Christ's Lordship
__ What I do reflects responsible stewardship
__ What I do is consistent with God's mission for me
__ What I do fits God's agenda and needs doing
__ What I do expresses my God given talents
__ What I do expresses my Spiritual gift(s)
__ What I do allows me to work with Christian integrity
__ What I do is based in the wisdom of God's Word

Building Your Self-Concept

A. Make a written contract with yourself to change:
   a. Be willing to invest in an ongoing effort
   b. Don't let set backs altar your commitment

B. Gain an understanding of the need for change:
   a. Know what changes are needed
   b. Know what will bring about the change
   c. Learn how to self disclose
   d. Learn how to manage conflict

C. Set realistic change goals as to how we will see ourselves:
   a. Create a supportive environment for change
      - Be with those who reflect positively and honestly of your self worth
      - Avoid those who reflect a negative attitude
      - Our self-communication must be positive and honest
   b. Develop an action step toward the goal of improving your self-image
   c. Pray for guidance and success
   d. Implement the action plan

LEVEL III
A. Who I am in relation to others - Social Systems:
   a. Family (Ephesians 5:22-6:4; Colossians 3:18-4:1)
   b. Work (Ephesians 6:5-9; Romans 13:1-10)
   c. Community (Luke 10)
B. James 5:16 NASB – "Therefore, confess your sins to one another, and pray for one another, so that you may be healed. The effective prayer of a righteous man can accomplish much."

Evaluate Social Relationships
(Ephesians 5:22-6:9; Colossians 3:18-4:1; 1 Peter 3:1-7)

WIVES	HUSBANDS	CHILDREN
Do you respect the authority of your husband?	Do you provide for your family in accordance with resources given?	How do you honor your mother and father?
How do you respect your husband?	How do you love your wife as yourself?	Do you obey in all lawful matters?
Do you submit in lawful matters?	How do you love your wife as Christ loves the Church?	How does what you do for your parent(s) please the Lord?
Are you one with your husband?	Are you one with your wife?	
Are you unreasonable with the children?	Do you exasperate or embitter your children?	
Is your relationship fitting as unto the Lord?	Are you following Christ?	
	How do you treat your wife with respect?	

Read the Scriptures and evaluate your social relationships based on your understanding of the Scriptures.

C. Submission in Relationships:
   a. Does not equal inferior
      - Jesus Christ – submissive to parents (Luke 2:51)
      - Obedience (Hebrew 13:17)
        - leaders will account to God for how they exercised authority
        - obedience should provide joy in work
   b. Voluntary subjection to God (James 4:7)
   c. Christian submission to one another in reference to Christ. (Ephesians 5:21)
      - Surrender personal interest to the interest of others
      - Provide service (1 Corinthians 16:15-16)
   d. Situational Submission:
      - Not based on justice/injustice
      - Not based on right/wrong
        - Student/teacher
        - Superior/subordinate
        - 1 Peter 2:13-3:7

BELIEVERS	**SUBORDINATES (Christians)**	**WIVES (Christians)**	**HUSBANDS (Christians)**
Obey authority, which punishes as well as that which commends.	Subject yourself to authority.	Subject yourself to your husband to win over the unbeliever.	Subject yourself and be considerate to your wife.
Do not authorize rebellion for evil.	Show respect for superiors.		Show respect, to do otherwise will hinder your prayers (block your blessings).
Show proper respect for all persons.	Your actions should be commendable to God.		
Remember all are made in His Image.	Actions should be examples of Christ.		

Work Relationships: (Ephesians 5:22-6:9; Colossians 3:22-4:1)

EMPLOYEE	EMPLOYER
Are you doing your job honestly at all times?	Are you authoritarian with your employees?
Are you doing your job simply to win favor?	Are you right and fair with your employees knowing you have a Master in heaven?
Are you doing your job with sincerity as in working for the Lord?	Do you unfairly threaten your employees?
Is it the Lord you are serving?	Do you serve your employees?

Read the Scriptures and apply the chart to your situation or to those of persons you know.

Describe your work environment.

- e. Community Relationships (Romans 13:1-10):
  - How do I value others?
    - subjection to governing authorities
    - tax to whom tax is due
    - custom to whom custom is due
    - honor to whom honor is due
    - owe nothing to any one except to love one another
    - love your neighbor as yourself
      - No adultery
      - No murder
      - No stealing
      - No coveting
    - Love does no wrong to a neighbor
    - Who is my neighbor (Luke 10)
  - Luke 10: 30-37
    - The self-righteous attitude does not build self-esteem or community relations
      - self-righteous attitude entraps
      - the lawyer seeking to trap Jesus about the greatest commandment

- The parable of the Good Samaritan
  - road of Jerusalem and Jericho
    - known for crime
    - road many seek to avoid
  - Jewish traveler robbed and left for dead
  - two Jewish (kinsmen) religious leaders go around
  - the one least likely to stop-the Samaritan
    - animosity between Jews and Samaritans
    - Samaritan shows compassion
  - the religious leaders, attitude of fear
  - religious leaders attitude of self concern
    - attitude causes division
    - attitude creates mistrust
    - attitude prevents relationships from building
    - leaders forgot who created them
    - leaders forgot how they got safe passage
    - leaders remain victims of worldly circumstances
    - leaders were not victors of the kingdom
  - Samaritan exercised freedom to follow God's Will
    - Choice to put aside animosity
    - Choice to show compassion
    - Choice to be used to heal
    - Choice to be used to provide shelter
  - the Samaritan remembered who he was
  - the Samaritan remembered where he was spiritually going
- Jonah called to be used of God:
  - preach salvation to a dying people
  - Jonah's anger caused his entrapment
  - Jonah's anger had historical rationale
    - Ninevah was the capital of Assyria
    - Assyria defeated and destroyed Israel
    - Ninevah described in the Book of Nahum as "city of Blood, never without victims"
- Jonah nourished an attitude of anger.
  - Jonah had a spirit of rebellion.
  - Jonah was entrapped to having to plea for his life.

- read the book of Jonah:
    - Why was Jonah in the belly of a large fish? (Jonah 1:1-17)
    - Is this place (wherever you may be) your large fish? Why? Why not?
    - What was the attitude of Jonah? (Jonah 2:1-4)
    - Where did Jonah look for help?
    - What action did Jonah take?
    - When did you last repent and pray?
    - When Jonah was released, what did he do?
    - When you are released, what will you do?

Where are you going with your life? Romans 6:22-23 (NASB) "But now having been freed from sin and enslaved to God, you derive your benefit, resulting in sanctification, and the outcome, eternal life. For the wages of sin is death, but the free gift of God is eternal life in Christ Jesus our Lord."

SELF-ASSESSMENT OF LEVEL III RELATIONSHIPS

__ I provided needed resources	__ I assist others to achieve goals
__ I am honest in my dealings	__ I identify talents in others
__ I trouble shoot problems	__ I respect different opinions
__ I borrow from _____	__ I lend to _____
__ I minister to my enemies	__ I share my knowledge and skills
__ I pray for friends	__ I pray for foes

Chapter 3
THE VICTIM MENTALITY

(VICTIM OR VICTOR?)

BSJ Christian Seminars
Minister Brenda Simuel Jackson, Ph.D.
© 2007 All rights reserved.

VICTORY
©2008 Brenda Simuel Jackson

Victory is my game, being a victim only brings shame.

Victory is my gift from Jesus, He is the one who loves me and leads us.

Victory allows me to fall and to rise, being a victim only allows losing what is wise.

Valuable lessons are learned on the victory road.

Valued experiences are to be told.

In my victory there is no condemnation, only a victim is found wrong because of fleshly relations.

The song says victory is mine, I will guard it with humility.

But a victim, I will resist becoming through Him who set me free.

SEMINAR OBJECTIVES

- Identify self-defeating attitudes
- Break the victim mentality
- Avoid the self-pity syndrome
- Achieve Spiritual acceptance

VICTIM MENTALITY
A. Self-Perception:
   a. feeling tied to the past
   b. attitude of being the target
   c. using self-justification to find sympathy
   d. using self-justification to seek actions on behalf of self
   e. God seems far away
   f. attitude of self-pity
   g. mentality of bondage
B. Chuck Colson: Book, *Life Sentence*:
   a. After release always felt singled out.,
   b. Society always seeking to blame him for something,
   c. His past dictating his present and future,
   d. Allowed self to be put in doldrums.
C. Victim or Victor?
   a. Who are you?
      - Past/present
      - What is your attitude?
      - How does your attitude affect your behavior?
      - Who guides your attitude?
      - What mental habits are not under control of the Holy Spirit?
        - Angry with self?
        - Blaming the system for your circumstances?
        - Fear a future of failure?
        - Fear of not being accepted?
      - 2 Corinthians 5:17: "Therefore, if anyone is in Christ, he is a new creation old things have passed away, behold all things have become new."
      - How do we see ourselves with our physical surroundings?
        - Victim or
        - Victor?
      - How do we see ourselves at this point in our lives?
        - Victim or
        - Victor?

- How do we see ourselves in daily routines?
  - Victim or
  - Victor?

- Victim-gram/Victor-gram:
  - Describe the following relationships as a victim:
    - Faith relationships
    - Parental relationships
    - Sibling relationships
    - Spousal/Significant other relationships
  - Describe the following relationships as a victor:
    - Faith relationships
    - Parental relationships
    - Sibling relationships
    - Spousal/Significant other relationships

- True Victim in scripture – Joseph:
  - Hated and rejected by his brothers (Genesis 37:1-27)
    - sold into bondage (37:28-36)
    - falsely accused of attempted rape (39:1—20)
    - forgotten in prison for over two years by one whom he had aided in his release (40:1-23)
  - Joseph's Attitude:
    - Accepted who he was and his condition
    - He did not play the blame game
    - He did exhibit self-pity
    - He did not seek self-justification
    - His mind remained clear
    - He became an overseer (39:2-6)
    - He resisted the opportunity to transgress against his captor and against God (39:8-10)
    - He followed the ways of the keeper of prison .
    - He became a leader (39:21)
    - After two years in prison, he came to the aid of Pharaoh (willingly)
    - He was used by God

- Analysis of Joseph's mental victory:
  - Joseph has _____ in the sight of the chief jailer
  - Why? _____
    Genesis 39:20-23
  - What kind of attitude did Joseph have? _____ Genesis 40:1-15
  - How can you get an attitude like Joseph? _____ Proverbs 3:1-8; Galatians 5:22-26
  - What good came from Joseph's imprisonment? Genesis 47:1-12, 50:15-21
  - What good will come from your imprisonment?
- Christ came to set you free:
  - freedom from the trap of sin
  - freedom from eternal damnation
  - freedom from physical traps
  - use you to help others to freedom
- Spiritual freedom is victory:
  - Self-pity is a form of pride.
  - the Holy Spirit brings understanding that we are not tied to this world.
    - freedom to stand for your faith (1 Corinthians 16:13)
    - freedom to conduct ourselves by the gospel (Philippians 1:27)
    - freedom to set our minds on heavenly things (Philippians 4)
    - freedom to live by the Spirit (Galatians 5:1)
    - freedom to know that there is no more condemnation (Romans 8:1)
    - freedom to produce good
    - freedom to serve God
    - freedom to practice the love of God
    - freedom to rely on God's grace
    - freedom to have the mind of Christ

- - - 1 Corinthians 2:16; 2 Corinthians 10:5-6
    - Having the mind of Christ is being obedient to His revelations: "casting down arguments and every high thing that exalts itself against the knowledge of God, bringing every thought into captivity to the obedience of Christ and being ready to punish all disobedience when your obedience is fulfilled."
- Knowing who you are:
  - Psalm 39:1-13 reminds us it is important to have Jesus as Lord:
  - Remember, we are finite
  - Remember, we cannot prolong our lives
  - Remember, we need God
    - Who knows the extent of your days? (Psalm 39:4)
    - Can riches prolong life? (39:6)
    - Who can sustain life? (39:7-11)
    - Does fellowship with God bring you joy? (39:12-13)
    - What should you be doing with your life?

MOTIVATION LADDER
(Adapted from Abraham Maslow's Hierarchy of Needs)

Ladder Position	Maslow's Hierarchy	God's Provisions
5	Self-Actualization	1 John 5:14-15: Being in the Will of God, purposeful living. 1 Corinthians 12:1-30: Spiritual Gifts. God given talents. Philemon 1:10-12: Being Useful Galatians 4:1-7, 31, 5:1: Set free
4	Self Esteem	Psalm 139:13-16: I am somebody. Genesis 1:26: I am made in the Image of God; Ephesians 2:1-9: I have been forgiven my sins; made alive I have been given what it takes to be successful as was Nehemiah, Paul, Timothy, Deborah, Lydia.
3	Love/Acceptance	John 3:16: God loves me. Ephesians 1:5; Roman 8:15; 9:4; Galatians 4:5: Adopted into the family of God, and joint heir with Jesus Christ. He will never forsake me. We have fellowship.
2	Safety/Security	Psalm 61:3-4, Provides refuge II Timothyothy 1:7: Provides power and sound mind and judgment, Philippians 4:7: Gives peace of mind. Ephesians 1:4: Security in our salvation.
1	Physiological	Manna, water at Meribah, physical healing. Today was with Christ and Paul, jobs, education, and training.

Complete each thought by supplying the missing word.
What motivates me?
- I need to _____.
- I could _____ every day and not get bored.
- I must _____ in order to be happy.
- When I am doing _____, I never notice the time.
- Without _____, I cannot exercise joy.
- I want to go _____.
- I want _____ type of benefits.

Prioritize each of your answers according to the hierarchy of needs as compared to God's hierarchy of meeting needs.

BIBLIOGRAPHY

BIBLES

Barker, Kenneth, (Ed). *NIV Study Bible, New International Version.* Grand Rapids, MI: Zondervan Publishing, 1985.

Scofield, C.I. (Ed). *The Scofield Study Bible, New King James Version.* Nashville: Thomas Nelson Publishers, 1989.

Thompson, Frank Charles. (Ed). *The Thompson Chain-Reference Bible. New American Standard Version.* USA: Kirkbride Bible Co., 1988.

COMMENTARIES

Richard, Lawrence O. *The Teacher's Commentary.* England: Victor Books, 1987.

Walvoord, John F. et al. *The Bible Knowledge Commentary, An exposition of the Scriptures by Dallas Seminary Faculty, N.T., O.T.* Chariot Victor Publishing, 1983.

REFERENCES

Boulding, Kenneth E. *The Image.* Ann Arbor, MI: University of Michigan, 1971.

Colson, Charles W. *Life Sentence.* New Jersey: Fleming H. Revell Co., 1979.

Hunt, June. *Counseling Through The Bible.* Hope for the Heart, Dallas, TX: 2004.

McGee, Robert S. *Search for Significance.* Life Support Edition. Nashville, TN: Life Way Press, 1992.

Munroe, Myles. *Maximizing your Potential.* Shippensburg, PA: Destiny Image Publishers, Inc. 2001.

Patterson, Gerald. *Families.* Champaign, IL: Research Press, 1971.

Sherrer, Quin and Garlock, Ruthanne. *A Woman's Guide To Breaking Bondages.* Ann Arbor, MI: Servant Publication, 1994.

Wood, Julia T. *Interpersonal Communication.* Everyday Encounters, (3rd ed). Wadsworth Learning, 2002.

Williams, Joseph. *Sheep In Wolves Clothing.* Chicago, IL: Moody Press, 2000.

Jensen, Irving L. *Jensen's Bible Study Charts,* "Galatians, Set Free From Bondage", Chicago: Moody Bible Institute, 1981, chart 58.

Staub, Dick and Trautman, Jeff. *Intercristo's Career Kit, A Christian's Guide to Career Building.* Seattle, WA: Intercristo 1997

Chapter 4
SHEEP OR GOAT?

DISCIPLE OR MANIPULATOR
(Mentor/Student Relationship)

BSJ Christian Seminars
Minister Brenda Simuel Jackson, Ph.D.
© 2006 All rights reserved.

A DISCIPLE AM I
©2008 Brenda Simuel Jackson

I am a disciple constantly seeking.

I am a disciple knowledge forever needing.

I am a disciple with a teachable spirit.

I am a disciple hoping to share my legacy wit.

I am a disciple; Jesus is my Lord, Whom I seek to obey.

I am a disciple of Jesus; He guides my way.

Although a disciple, I at times do stray.

These are the times forgive me I seriously pray.

Who are you, you say?

SEMINAR OBJECTIVES

- Learn why one should have a Spiritual Mentor

- Learn how to be an effective Disciple/Mentee

- Learn to discern when there is manipulation in the mentor/student relationship

- Learn to adopt a Disciple's attitude

SCRIPTURES

Psalm 23:1-4

Luke 6:39-40

II Timothyothy 2:15-17a

1 Thessalonians 2:3-6a

I. The Role of a Mentor
   A. Trusted Counselor
   B. Trusted Guide
   C. Tutor
   D. Coach
   E. 1st Timothy 1 - 2nd Timothy 4:22 To Timothy, my dear son:
      1. Paul probably led Timothy to Christ
      2. Timothy accompanied Paul on his missionary journeys
      3. Timothy shared in evangelization
      4. Timothy was with Paul on Paul's preaching ministry
      5. Timothy was with Paul during Paul's imprisonment
      6. Timothy represented Paul
      7. Paul encouraged Timothy in Timothy's ministry
      8. Paul warned Timothy of dangers to come

What was the motive of Timothy? Of Paul?
Describe the attitude of Timothy.

II. The Needs of The Student:
   A. Psalm 23:1-4
      1. Shepherd and The Sheep
      2. Images of a sheep in the care of a shepherd
   B. Sheep
      1. In ancient Middle East, precious symbols of wealth.
      2. In Scripture, a metaphor for humanity.
      3. Dependent creatures
      4. Need guidance.
         a. Guidance for food.
         b. Guidance for water.
      5. Need protection
   C. Psalm 23:1
      1. Sheep recalls the blessings enjoyed from the Shepherd (The Lord)
      2. Metaphor of a teacher/mentor - instruction is being blessed

D. Psalm 23:2a
   1. The first blessing, David experienced was spiritual nourishment.
   2. Nourishment from your mentor
      a. Mental - Bible study
      b. Emotional - prayer life
      c. Physical - financial stewardship
      d. Spiritual - faith

E. Psalm 23:2b-3a
   1. The second blessing that comes from the Lord - spiritual restoration - forgiveness
   2. A mentor helps restore relationships
      a. With God
      b. With Family
      c. With Community

F. Psalm 23:3b
   1. The third blessing is guidance in paths of righteousness - safety.
   2. A mentor/teacher shows the correct way.
      a. Obedience to God
      b. Obedience to the Law
      c. Obedience to those in authority.

G. Psalm 23:4
   1. The fourth blessing is protection.
   2. Teacher/mentor instructs through unknown circumstances
      a. Job seeking
      b. Budget making
      c. Church finding

III. Describe five (5) characteristics of yourself as a sheep in need of a shepherd:

Samples:
A. I am like a sheep in need of a shepherd because I
_____

B. I am like a sheep in need of a shepherd when I
_____

IV. Poor Discipleship:
   A. The Manipulator
      1. Control of a person for personal motives or advantage
      2. Use of unfair methods to gain influence
      3. Doing things to get one's own way
      4. Genesis 25:27-34
         a. Esau and Jacob
         b. Jacob withheld physical nourishment to gain advantage over Esau
      5. 2 Samuel 13:1-14
         a. Amnon used deception with his father, David to get an opportunity to exploit his sister
         b. Ruined his sister's future
      6. Judges 16:15
         a. Delilah used mental pressure to manipulate Sampson
         b. Used repeatedly to wear Sampson down
   B. A manipulator uses guile, bait, and a snare.
   C. A manipulator is out for profit at any cost.
   D. A manipulator has impure motives.
   E. A manipulator uses flattery to cover up for covetousness.

1 Thessalonians 2:3-6a NIV
For the appeal we make does not spring from error or impure motives, nor are we trying to trick you. On the contrary, we speak as men approved by God to be entrusted with the gospel. We are not trying to please men, but God, who tests our hearts. You know we never used flattery, nor did we put on a mask to cover up greed.

V. The Manipulator is not a sheep but a goat.
    A. Goats are hardy and able to survive in arid regions.
        1. They overgraze
        2. They eat roots of the plants
    B. Goats are related to sheep.
    C. Metaphor for a licentious person who has no regard for rules.
    D. Metaphor for one who has no regard for restraints.
    E. Symbolically, the goat represents sin and condemnation.
    F. Describe 5 characteristics of yourself as an unrestrained goat.

Sample:
1. I am like a goat when I _____.
2. I am like a goat because I _____.

VI. The Goal of a mentor relationship: Luke 6:39-40; Luke 39-40 NIV
    A. "Can a blind man lead a blind man? Will they not both fall into a pit?"
    B. "A student is not above his teacher, but everyone who is fully trained will be like his teacher."
    C. What are your motives for seeking a mentor relationship?
        1. The goal of discipleship was that the learner would not only master what the teacher knew, but become like the teacher in belief and standards.
        2. Learn by practical experience.
        3. Learn through instruction.

VII. Biblical Mentor/Disciple Relationships
    A. Ruth and Naomi (Ruth 1:1 -4:12)
        1. Ruth is the Disciple
            a. Committed
            b. Loyalty
            c. Love
        2. Ruth expected no material gain in return
    B. Elijah and Elisha (2 Kings 2:2, 4-6)
        1. Elisha would not leave his mentor
        2. Elisha sought the spirit of his teacher
        3. Elisha had an attitude of perseverance, and commitment

- C. Joshua and Moses (Numbers 14:1-6, Deuteronomy 34:9)
    1. Joshua was faithful to God
    2. Joshua gained in wisdom
- D. Timothy and Paul
    1. Sincere Faith (II Timothy 1:4)
    2. Confidence (II Timothy 1:7)
    3. Love
    4. Self-discipline
    5. Not ashamed to live a godly life. (II Timothy 1:8-10)
    6. Remembered sound teaching learned (II Timothy 1:13-14)
    7. Avoided stupid arguments (II Timothy 2:24)
    8. Learned to endure hardships (II Timothy 2:3)
    9. Followed the rules (II Timothy 2:5)

VIII. Write a vision statement for a Mentor Disciple Relationship

Chapter 5
VALUING DIVERSITY

BSJ Christian Seminars
Minister Brenda Simuel Jackson, Ph.D.
© 2007 All rights reserved.

DIFFERENCES, DO THEY MATTER?
©2004 Brenda Simuel Jackson

Does it matter that we are different?

I am Black and you are not.

I am old and you are young.

Does it really matter that we are different?

I have degrees, and you have one.

Does it matter truly, that we are different?

I was born in the mid-west, you in the South;

Does it matter that you can walk and I can't,

I can hear, and you don't.

Does it matter, I an rich in Spirit, you in silver and gold?

Does it make a difference?

Only if we look from a different point of view.

SEMINAR OBJECTIVES

- Understanding the Biblical principles regarding diversity
- Understand how Jesus Christ represents and respects differences.
- Understanding the meaning of diversity.

DIVERSITY

I. What is Diversity?
Diversity is "The degree of basic human differences among a given population." (Samuel C. Certo, *Modern Management,* Prentice Hall, 1997, 565)

II. Areas of Diversity
   A. Age
   B. Beliefs
   C. Cultures/Customs
   D. Education
   E. Ethnicity
      1. Various racial groups of people and characteristics of language and customs.
      2. Various cultural groups
      3. Various nationalities
   F. Family Structure
   G. Gender
   H. Geographic Location
   I. Language
   J. Physical Ability
   K. Race
   L. Religion
   M. Social Class
   N. Talents

THE BIBLICAL ORIGIN OF DIVERSITY[1]

I. Following the Fall of Man, it was God's intent that there be one family, His family.

   A. Genesis 12:2-3 NIV is a promise to Abraham which states, I will make you into a great nation and I will bless you; ...all the peoples [families] on earth will be blessed through you.

   B. The families of Abraham were of three groups.
1. Ishmael - The Arab Race
2. Israel - The Israelites
3. Other Semitic peoples - Born of Keturah, Abraham's second wife or his concubine. (1 Chronicles 1:32-33, Genesis 25:1-4)

   C. Family within the Old and New Testament is the basic unit of the believing community.

   D. Family is the basis for the "Third Dispensation (Post Flood), Human Government.

II. The Church is a family and the common cord is one Father, with shared beliefs. (Ephesians 3:16-19)

---

[1] Thompson, Alfred, S.T.D., *The Panorama Bible Study Course*, New Jersey: Fleming H. Revell Co., 1947, and Richards, Lawrence, O. *The Revell Bible Dictionary.* New Jersey: Fleming H. Revell, 1984.

BIBLICAL ORIGINS OF DIVERSITY

I. After the Flood, there was one family, Noah, His wife, his sons, and their wives.

   A. Genesis 9:1, Then God blessed Noah and his sons, saying to them, "Be Fruitful and increase in number and fill the earth." (NIV)

   B. The Sons of Noah were the fathers of various families that peopled the earth.
      1. Ham had four sons that fathered nations
      2. Shem had six sons that fathered nations
      3. Japheth had seven sons that fathered nations

   C. The language of the world was made diverse.
      1. Genesis 11:1 "Now the whole world had one language and a common speech."
      2. Genesis 11:5 "But the Lord came down to see the city and the tower that the men were building."
      3. Genesis 11:6 "If as one people speaking the same language they have begun to do this, then nothing they plan to do will be impossible for them."
      4. Genesis 11:7 "Come, let us go down and confuse their language so they will not understand each other."
      5. Genesis 11:9c "From there the Lord scattered them over the face of the whole earth."

BIBLICAL ORIGIN OF DIVERSITY

Sons of Noah	Descendants of Noah's Sons	Nations	Geographic Locations	Scriptures	Anthropological and Biblical Concepts
HAM	Cush	Ethiopians (Cushites, Nubians)	Africa Arabia Ethiopia is not the same as modern day Ethiopia.	Genesis 11:1-9; Isaiah 18:2,7	Location was along the upper Nile. "Isaiah spoke of the Ethiopians as "A people tall and smooth skinned...feared far and wide, an aggressive nation of strange speech.
	Mizraim	Egyptians	Egypt	Genesis 10:6,13 Isaiah 19:25; Jeremiah 46.	Developed around the Nile River "The prophets warn that Egypt will be punished, but the Lord will bless Egypt.
	Phut	Libyans	North Africa to the West of Egypt	Genesis 10:13; 2 Chronicles 12:3; Nahum 3:9; Acts 2:10	
	Canaan	Phoenicians and Canaanites, Jebusites, Amorites, Girgasite, Hivite, etc.	Northeast of Palestine, Principal cities are Sidon and Tyre in the Old Testament.	Mark 7:26 Acts 11:19 Genesis 10:15-20	Settled in the 4th Millennium B.C. by the same people who occupied Canaan. Planted colonies in Spain, Morocco, and Algeria.

Sons of Noah	Descendants	Nations	Geographic Locations	Scriptures	Anthropological and Historical Concepts.
SHEM	Arphaaxad	(Hebrew Race) Assyria Persians, Assyrians, Chaldeans, Armenians Syrain	Mesopotamia lying between the Tigris and Euphrates (Fertile Crescent)	Genesis 10:11; 2 Kings 15-19;Ezekial 16:28	Defeated the Northern Kingdom of Israel, Ninevah was the Capitol.
	ABRAM	The Arab Race Edomites The Israelites; the families of Katurah	Egypt; Edom, Mountainous territory, south of Moab Canaan Country of Judea	Joshua 15:52; 2 Samual 8:13,14; 2 Kings 8:20-22, Jeremiah 49:7-22.	God's Chosen Peoples; dispersed.
JEPHETH	Gomer, Madai, Tubal, Tiras, Magog, Javan, Meschech	Gauls, Britons, Germans, Russians, Medes, Iberians, Greeks, Romans, Thracians.	Asia Minor and Europe		

GENTILES

I. Gentile is a non-Jewish individual or people

   A. The rights of resident aliens protected although emphasis was on separation of Hebrew and Non-Hebrew.

   B. The Gospel message is to the Jew and the Gentile.

   C. All barriers between Jew and Gentile were broken. (Ephesians 2:11-22)

II. All persons have access to God through Jesus Christ. (Acts 10:34-35, 43; Romans 12:11, 10:13)

THE CHRISTIAN AND DIVERSE CULTURES

I. Culture is permitted by an all-knowing God
   A. The culture of Christ
      1. The Bible is authoritative in all matters
      2. Culture is measured by God's Word
         a. Some components of different cultures are wholesome and do not violate God's Word
         b. Some components of different cultures do not violate God's Word and would be an improvement through change

   B. The culture of Satan
      1. Some components violate God's Word such as idolatry and would not be adopted
      2. Some components of culture worship a spirit other than the Spirit of God

   C. Issues of cross cultural communication[2]
      1. Worldviews - Ways of perceiving the world
      2. Cognitive Processes - Ways of thinking
      3. Linguistic Forms - Ways of expressing ideas
      4. Behavioral Patterns - Ways of acting

---

[2] Hesselgrave, David J. *Communicating Christ Cross-Culturally (2nd ed)*. Grand Rapids: Zondervan Publishing House, 1991, pp 161 - 173.

5. Social Structures - Ways of interacting (Codes of Conduct)
6. Media Influence - Ways of channeling the message
7. Motivational Resources - Ways of deciding

BIBLICAL FOUNDATION OF DIVERSITY

SCRIPTURES	WHO	CONTEXT/SETTING	APPLICATION
1 Corinthians 9:19-22	Paul, Apostle to the Gentiles	Paul describes his witness, "For though I am free from all men, I have made myself a slave to all, so that I may win more…to the Jews I became as a Jew…to those under the law, as under the law…to the weak I became weak…I have become all things to all men, so that I may by all means save some." (NASB)	Understanding a person's differences is perceived better when as Paul you take on some of the characteristics. This will improve the relationship and make you a better witness to that person. Paul valued the person and the goal (his/her salvation) that he was seeking.
1 Corinthians 12:4-10	Paul	Paul demonstrates how the Holy Spirit has equipped each person with different gifts and ministries. Even though the gifts are different, the goal is the same. The source of the gifts are the same source, the same Spirit, the same Lord. If differences were not present, the organism would not function.	As with a team, Scripture shows us that our Lord values diversity and expects the body to have diverse units, not everything is homogenous, although we are one unit. There is one source, the God Head. Whatever gift is given, it can be used in the same manner or the same way, but the goal is the same. In valuing diversity, we must keep the goal in sight. Unity of diversity is the source of the gift(s), and is the goal of using the gift(s).
1 Corinthians 12:11-13	Paul	Our differences in our gifts are not by our decision but by the source of the gifts, but all are members of the same body.	As members of the body [team], all are important; no one is better than the other. There is a mutual dependence. If the gift (skill) is important, then there is a need for the person to exhibit the gift which he/she has been blessed with.
1 Corinthians 12:15-24a	Paul	Within the Christian body there should not be a division, there should not be jealousy over the abilities of another, and there should be concern and care for one another. If one member suffers, all the members suffer.	Valuing diversity is working together as a unit to achieve common goals.

SCRIPTURES	WHO	CONTEXT/SETTING	APPLICATION
1 Corinthians 13:1-13	Paul	Paul warns us not to think more highly of ourselves than we ought as we perform our gifts in proportion to the faith given to us.	The basis for accepting the various gifts that we all have is the gift of love which helps us to value the differences in others. Showing patience demonstrates value.
Romans 12:3-8	Paul	Paul; warns not to think more highly of ourselves than we ought as we perform our gifts in proportrion to the faith given to us.	Humility is a way to learn to value diversity.
James 2:1-4; 8-9	James, Head of Church in Jerusalem, and half biological brother of Jesus Christ.	James tells us that the Lord did not distinguish between the rich and the poor regarding who would receive faith and salvation. Those in Christ have wisdom and use it without partiality, and without hypocrisy.	Differences can lead to unity and not separation. We are to value the intrinsic things of a person and not the material things that the person may own.
Acts 10:1-48	Luke, the Physician, and Researcher, a Greek, non-Jewish, Missionary	The Lord prepares Peter to minister to a Roman Officer who was an Italian. It was unlawful for a Jew to associate with a foreigner or to visit him, but God showed Peter that he could not call any man unholy or unclean. He states in vv 34-36, "I most certainly understand now that God is not one to show partiality, but in every nation the man who fears Him and does what is right is welcome to Him." Cornelius had others in his home when Peter visited, they may have included Britons, Spaniards, Slavs, Germans, Greeks as well as Italians. Soldiers were drafted from these different groups.	Valuing diversity means association, and fellowship, and ministering to those who are different. Valuing differences is treating others as allies.

BIBLICAL FOUNDATION OF DIVERSITY cont'd

SCRIPTURES	WHO	CONTEXT/SETTING	APPLICATION
Isaiah 2:2-4	Prophet Isaiah	Isaiah is telling Judah of what will happen in the last days. He stresses all nations will be affected, and as many peoples who come to the Lord will be saved.	God's promise is to His whole creation, not just one race or ethnic groups. God's original promise to Abraham says, "All the people of the earth will be blessed through His covenant People."
Jonah 1:1-4:11	Jonah	Jonah was sent to a non-Jewish nation, Ninevah, to warn them of God's pending wrath.	God showed His concern for the non-Jew. We should follow the example.
Ruth 1:1-4:22	Ruth	Ruth was a Moabite, non-Jew, who was accepted into the Jewish nation, and whose son is in the lineage of Jesus Christ.	God showed His concern for the non-Jew. We should follow the example.
2 Kings 5:1-14	Naaman	Naaman was a soldier who was a non-Jew that the Lord healed from Leprosy...	God showed His concern for the non-Jew. We should follow the example.
Acts 8:14-25	Luke	Jesus goes to Samaria to those who were despised and rejected. The Samaritans were a mixed people as a result of the Assyria invasion and conquest. In John 4:9, the statement is made, "Jews do not associate with Samaritans. Jesus simply said, "I must need go to Samaria." In Samaria, He met the woman at the well and offered her life through the Holy Sspirit.	The love of Jesus did not discriminate, the value of all men is for God's glory, and we must treat and value all for the Glory of God.

DIVERSITY CHECK LIST

To assess how hard you will have to work to effectively work in a diverse group, rate yourself on your responses to the statements below. Use a scale of 1 to 5 to rate how strongly you agree with the statements. 1 is low agreement; and 5 is high agreement.

___1. I regularly assess my strengths and weaknesses, and I consciously try to improve myself.

___2. I am interested in the ideas of people who do not think as I think, and I respect their opinions even when I disagree with them.

___3. Some of my friends or associates are different from me in age, race, gender, physical abilities, economic status, and education.

___4. If I were at a party with people outside of my own group, I would go out of my way to meet them.

___5. I do not need to understand everything going on around me. I tolerate ambiguity.

___6. I am able to change course quickly. I readily change my plans or expectations to adapt to a new situation.

___7. I recognize that I am a product of my upbringing, and my way is not the only way.

___8. I am patient and flexible. I can accept different ways of getting a job done as long as the results are good.

___9. I am always asking questions, reading, and exploring. I am curious about new things, people and places.

___10. I am interested in human dynamics and often find myself thinking, "What's really going on here?"

___11. I can see two sides on most issues.

___12. I have made mistakes, and I have learned from them.

___13. In an unfamiliar situation, I watch and listen before acting.

___14. I listen carefully.

___15. When I am lost, I ask for directions.

___16. When I don't understand what someone is saying, I ask for clarification.

___17. I sincerely do not want to offend others.

___18. I like people and accept them as they are.

___19. I am sensitive to the feelings of others and observe their reactions when I am talking.

___20. I am aware of my prejudices and consciously try to control my assumptions about people.

How to score: Total your answers. If your score is 80 or above, you probably value diversity and are able to work with people who are different from yourself, but you certainly have room for improvement. If your score is below 50, you probably experience much difficulty working with a diverse group and could benefit from in-depth Bible Study on the subject and training. (Adapted from the Diversity Plan of Northville State Hospital, 1998)

CULTURAL DISTANCE

The following is an exercise to measure your cultural distance from another participant in the group.

As a Christian/Non-Christian, you define drunkenness as inappropriate behavior. Put your initials in the square that best represents where you stand in relation to Biblical Culture and World Culture.

Add your score by adding the numbers of the column in which you have placed your initials. The Lowest total number for Biblical Culture is 7 and the highest total number indicating World culture is 70.

CULTURAL COMMUNICATION ITEM	Biblical Culture									World Culture
	1	2	3	4	5	6	7	8	9	10
World View										
Cognitive Processes										
Linguistic Form										
Behavioral Pattern										
Social Structure										
Media Influence										
Motivational Influence										

TOTAL DISTANCE: _____

BIBLIOGRAPHY

BIBLES

Barker, Kenneth. (Gen Ed.). *The NIV Study Bible.* Grand Rapids, MI: Zondervan Bible Publishers, 1985.

Scofield, C.I. (Ed.). *New Scofield Study Bible, New King James Version.* Nashville, TN: Thomas Nelson Publishers, 1989.

Thompson, Frank Charles, (Ed.). *The Thompson Chain – Reference Bible, New American Standard Version.* USA. Kirkbride, Bible Co., 1983.

MANUALS

Diversity Plan, Northville State Hospital, 1997.

Eade, Alfred Thompson. *The New Panorama Bible Study Course.* New Jersey: Fleming H. Revell Company, 1947.

BOOKS

Certo, Samuel C. *Modern Management: Diversity, Quality, Ethics, and the Global Environment,* (7th Ed.). New Jersey:Prentice-Hall, 1997.

Hasselgrave, David J. *Communicating Christ Cross-Culturally.* (2nd Ed.). Grand Rapids, MI: Zondervan Publishing House, 1991.

Mindel, Charles H., Habenstein, Robert W. & Wright, Jr., Roosevelt. *Ethnic Families in America.* (4th Ed.). New Jersey: Prentice Hall, 1988.

Moorhead, Gregory and Griffin, Ricky. *Organizational Behavior.* Boston, MA: Houghton Mifflin Co., 1990.

Richards, Lawrence O. *The Revell Bible Dictionary.* New Jersey; Fleming H. Revell Company, 1990.

Whetten, David A. and Cameron, Kim S. *Developing Management Skills.* (2nd Ed.) New York: Harper-Collins, 1991.

Chapter 6
GOING INTO LEADERSHIP

BSJ Christian Seminars
Minister Brenda Simuel Jackson, Ph.D.
© 2007 All rights reserved.

TO THE INCARCERATED – SEEK THE LEADER IN YOU
© 2007 Brenda Simuel Jackson

"For I know the plans I have for you," requires the exercise of the leadership talent that you can do.

"For I know the plans I have for you," You have gifts, why so down and blue?

"I know the plan I have for you," Although there may be failures, hope and prosperity are your due.

"I know the plans I have for you," don't worry, don't forget, where there is doubt, pray, and remember how you got to.

"I know the plans I have for you," follow Me, do My will, let My light shine through you, and your leadership will be *real*.

SEMINAR OBJECTIVES

- Identify your leadership style
- Identify effective leadership traits
- Understand Biblical characteristics of effective leadership
- Understand Scriptural support for a career
- Understand the theology of work

I. **Leadership Defined:**
   A. Leadership: Application of influence to develop people, to help people reach potential (John Maxwell)
   B. Leadership: Influence; the ability of one to influence others to follow (J. Oswald Sanders)
   C. Leadership: The act of making a difference (Hackman & Johnson)

II. **Leader Defined:**
   A. Leader: A person or something that guides
   B. Leader: The most significant position
   C. Leader: One who rules
   D. Biblical definition (Greek N.T.)
      1. Luke 6:39 - A leader is a teacher who bears fruit
      2. Matthew 15:14 - A leader is one who guides the way
      3. Hebrew 13:7, 24 - A leader is one who rules over; one who is imitated
      4. Acts 8:31 - A leader guides to understanding

III. **Leader Types**
   A. Positional
   B. Knowledge/expertise
   C. Charisma
   D. Appointment

IV. **What Type of Leader Are You?**
   A. Autocratic?
   B. Supervisory?
   C. Democratic?
   D. Participatory?
   E. Laissez faire?

LEADERSHIP STYLES
(Adapted from Lecture Notes, 2002, Central Michigan University)

AUTHORITARIAN/ SUPERVISORY	DEMOCRATIC/ PARTICIPATIVE	LAISSEZ-FAIRE
Sets goals individually Directs goal setting	Involves others in goal setting	Followers set own goals
One way communication	Open communication	Superficial communication
Controls discussions	Facilitates discussion	Avoids discussion
Dominates interaction/guides interaction	Focuses interaction	Avoids interaction
Personally directs tasks/provides oversight	Provides suggestions and alternatives	Input only as needed
Infrequent positive feedback	Frequent positive feedback	Infrequent feedback of any kind
Poor/average listener	Effective listener/positive climate	May have poor or effective listening skills
Uses conflict/competition for personal gain	Mediate conflict for mutual gain/encourages competition for mutual gain	Avoids conflict and competition
Rewards obedience, punishes mistakes	Rewards accomplishments, punish as last resort	Avoids rewards and punishments

V. Biblical Leaders (Examples)

    A. Abram

    B. Moses

    C. Deborah

    D. Paul

    E. Esther

    F. Nehemiah

    G. Timothy

SCRIPTURE CONTEXT	LED BY GOD	FAITH FACTOR	OCCUPATION	SPECIAL TRAINING	LEADER ROLE	CHARACTERISTICS
Genesis 12:1-4, 13:1-2, 8-9, 14:1-2 God's call to Abram Battle with Kings of Sodom and Gomorrah, and separation from Lot	ABRAM	Obedient to the Call	Rich Herdsman in livestock, silver, and gold		Led his family from Ur; Led the battle which rescued Lot against the King of Zeboim.	Obedient to God's leading Leader in battle Through discussion maintained family relations with Lot
Exodus 3:1-14, 4:10-16, 12:1-50, 18:1-27 Moses selected to lead God's people from bondage Moses receives advise from his Father-in-Law	MOSES	Obedient to the Call	Prince, herdsman, and prophet	Kings training, 40 years in the desert	Prophet, judge, negotiator, instructor	Persevering, slow speaker, impetuous, obedient to God's leading, concern for the followers, and accepts advise
Judges 4:1-13, Deborah gives Barak his orders from God. She is God's prophetess, and judge. She encourages Barak for war	DEBORAH	Delivered God's messages	Prophetess, wife, and judge		Judged Israel, Like a Secretary of State for Barak.	Accurately delivered God's message, willing to go where the followers are sent
Acts 27:39-28:17 Paul is shipwrecked on the way to Rome	PAUL	Obedient to God's call and work for him.	Tent maker, teacher, previous persecutor of Christians	Taught by Gamaliel, A respected teacher, had a trade, and spoke 14 different languages	Kept those on the ship together, was used as an instrument to save lives	Obedient to God's revelation An encourager of the followers Set an example for the followers to follow, a preacher

Leaders Used by God

(Examples)

SCRIPTURES	LEADER	CHARACTERISTICS
Esther 4:1-5:8	Esther	Prayer, risk taker, believer, put others first
Nehemiah 1:1-5:19	Nehemiah	Prayer, believer, fasted, planner, bold in request, empathy with the people, goal setting oriented in getting the wall built
1 Timothy 1:18-20, 2:6	Timothy	Young, Schooled by his mother, grandmother, and Paul; followed Paul, committed, and faithful believer.

How would you characterize the leadership style of these forefathers/mothers?

VI. Predominant Style of Jesus
   A. Humble

   B. Taught by example

   C. Democratic/ Participative
      1. Involved followers
      2. Open communication
      3. Facilitated discussion
      4. Focused interaction
      5. Frequent feedback
      6. Effective listener

John 13:12-17 (NIV)
"When he had finished washing their feet, he put on his clothes and returned to his place. Do you understand what I have done for you?...You call me 'Teacher' and 'Lord' and rightly so, for that is what I am. Now that I, your Lord and Teacher, have washed your feet, you also should wash one another's feet. I have set you an

example that you should do as I have done for you." I tell you the truth, no servant is greater than his master, nor is a messenger greater than the one who sent him."

D. Seminar participants provide examples of Christ's leadership style, - an example is the woman caught in adultery.

E. If setting permits, have a mock foot washing worship. Water is not necessary.

VII. Minimum Level of Skills for Respected Leadership

A. Communication

B. Accountability

C. Trust

D. Clarity of Vision

E. Sharing of Information

F. Joint Problem-Solving

G. Level of Expertise

H. Knowledge of Weaknesses

I. Not ashamed to seek help (includes Spiritual guidance)

Communication Skills
- Moses: Exodus 4:10-16
- Minimal Skills
    - Interpersonal
    - Listening
    - Public Speaking
    - Group/Conference Techniques
    - Use of Technology
    - Writing
    - Reading

Communication:
James 1:19-24 Leaders listen
- Swift to hear

- Slow to speak
- Slow to wrath

James 3:3-6 Leaders investigate and do not spread malicious gossip, rumors
- Do not gossip
- Do not spread rumors
- Sets the proper communication climate to support positive discussions

Proverbs 15:1-4, 18 Leaders choose their words wisely.
- Guard what you say.
- Select your words wisely
- do not be defensive

"A wrathful man stirs up strife, But he who is slow to anger allays contentions."

Accountability Skills:
I. Saul: 1 Samuel 15:10-111
II. Deborah & Barak: Judges 4:8-10
III. Answerable for Actions/Non actions
        A.   **Maintaining records**
        B.   **Reckoning transactions**
Accountability Skills
1 Samuel 15:10-11 (Saul is rejected as King)
"Now the word of the Lord came to Samuel, saying, 'I greatly regret that I have set up Saul as King, for he has turned back from following me, and has not performed my commandments and it grieved Samuel, and he cried out to the Lord all night.

Judges 4:8-10 (Barak is reluctant)
"And Barak said to her, "If you will go with me, then I will go; but if you will not go with me I will not go. So she said, 'I will surely go with you, nevertheless, there will be no glory for you in the journey you are taking, for the Lord will sell Sisera into the hands of a woman..."

Trustworthy Traits:

- Moses : Exodus 4:1-5
    i. Confidence in the person's intent
- Follow those in whom there is trust
    i. Credibility
    ii. Lack of suspicion
    iii. Freedom from fear to discuss
        1. Removal of perception of manipulation
        2. Removes attitude of aggression
        3. Removes uncertainty of outcome

Exodus 4:1-5 (The Lord is sending Moses on a mission, but Moses needs assurance that Israelites will believe him.)
Then Moses answered and said, "But suppose they will not believe me or listen to my voice, suppose they say, The Lord has not appeared to you...a rod...became a serpent...became a rod...they may believe that the Lord God of their fathers...has appeared to you. As the Lord is faithful, leaders must be faithful.

Clarity of Vision
- Habakkuh 2:2-3
    - Habakkuh has faith the vision, the revelation, will happen.
    - Leaders must have faith for future.
    - Write the vision, write the revelation, and engrave it so plainly upon tablets that everyone who passes may (be able to) read [it easily and quickly] as he hastens by. For the vision is yet for an appointed time, and it hastens to the end [to the fulfillment]; it will not deceive or disappoint. Through it tarry, wait (earnestly) for it, because it will sure come; it will not be behind hand on its appointed day. (Amplified)
- Clear Purpose
- Clear Commitment
- Clear Strategies of Achieving
- Clarity of beneficiaries of vision
- Biblical Visions

- o Ezekiel 37:1 – Ezekiel knew there was a future for Israel
- o The leader must see the future.
- o Isaiah 1:1 – Leader must have spiritual perception.
    - o Vision seen by Isaiah was Sppiritual.
- o 2 Chronicles 32:32 – Others need to see your vision.
- o The acts of Hezekiah written in vision of Isaiah the prophet
- o Revelations 1:10-11; 4:1

Information Sharing and Problem-solving Skills
- o Maintaining confidences , not hoarding information to gain power (gatekeeping)
    - o Ester 2:19-22
        - Knowing when to share information
        - Knowing with whom to share information
        - Critical for effective leadership
        - "Now Ester had not yet revealed her nationality or her people, for she obeyed Mordecai's command to her {to fear God and execute His commands] just as when she was being brought up by him. In those days, while Mordecai sat at the King's gate, two of the King's enunchs…sought to lay hands on King Ahaseurus…this was known to Mordecai who told it to Queen Esther, and Esther told the King in Mordecai's name.
    - o Proverbs 15:22-23
        - Plans fail for lack of counsel
        - With many advisors, plans succeed
        - A man finds joy in giving an apt reply
        - It is good when the word is timely
- o Leader must receive input from others who are effected by the decisions
    - o Proverbs 15:22-23
    - o Matthew 18:19-20: Jesus…Again, I tell you that if two of you on earth agree about anything you ask for, it will be done for you by my Father in heaven. For where two or three come together in my name, there I am with them.

- Matthew 18:18-19: Make sure decision of what is proper and improper, line up with God's instructions. – "Truly I tell you, whatever you forbid and declare to be improper and unlawful on earth must be what is already forbidden in heaven, and whatever you permit and declare proper and lawful on earth must be what is already permitted in heaven." (Amplified)
- 2 Corinthians 13:1: "…Every matter must be established by the testimony of two or three witnesses."

COMMUNICATION CLIMATE ~ PROVERBS 1:1 – 30:33

Scriptures	Supportive Communication Climate	Defensive, Negative Communication Climate
2:1-2,6	Seeks understanding	
4:1,10	Pays attention, Listens	
4:23		Perversity, corrupt talk
5:3		Smooth sounding deceptive talk
6:19		False witness, lies
10:11	Provides Wisdom	Provides Violence
10:14		Ruins Character
10:18		Spreads Slander
10:19		Produces Sin
10:20	Provides Value Added	
10:21	Is a helper	Leaves one helpless
11:13	Creates Trust	Negates Trust
12:6	Rescues the person	Destroys
12:20	Brings a closeness to God (His delight)	Causes separation from God (He detests)
13:2	Provides good results	Results in Violence
14:3	Protects	Causes Punishment
14:5		Causes deception
15:1	Causes Peace	Causes Anger
15:2	Brings Knowledge	Brings folly
15:4	Causes healing	Oppresses

15:28	Investigates responses	Speaks without thought
16:10	Brings justice	
16:23	Provides instruction	
16:27		Is inflammatory, and destructive
16:28		Separates Friends
17:4		Is malicious
17:20		Is deceitful, causes trouble
17:27-28	Uses silence and restraint	
18:6		Can Cause beatings
18:7		Is a trap for the soul
18:20,21	Meets physical needs	Can cause death
19:13		Causes irritation
21:23	Free from calamity	
22:21	Sound answers	
25:9		Shame, betrayal, bad reputation
25:12	Priceless Speech	
25:24		Separates husband and wife
26:20	Ends quarrels	
26:22		Causes constant indigestion
26:23-25		Is seductive, deceptive, abominable
29:11	Demonstrates Control	Vents anger

YOUR PERSONAL ATTRIBUTES

- Become an expert in your passion
- Foster genuineness
- Have a pleasant appearance
- Go the extra mile
- Perform symbolic acts of value

THE MASTER PLAN AND GOAL SETTING PROCESSES
- The Blue Print for Action
    - The Mission Statement
    - The team Members (Organization Chart0
    - The Recipients of the Products
- Characteristics of the Mission Statement
    - Describes service provided
    - Describes type of organization
    - Describes recipients of service
    - Describes nature/quality of service/product
    - Describes how to measure effectiveness
    - Sample Mission Statement: Christian Seminars for Prison Ministry: The mission is to build the gifts of the incarcerated through outreach ministry through the Holy Spirit's power to present the Gospel of Jesus Christ, and the plan of salvation to those who may not hear it because of incarceration, to provide a method of faith based involvement in rehabilitation of those who are confined, provide spiritual, personal, and academic development for those confined, provide mental health care giving to help persons in crisis to improve interpersonal relationship with God, self, and others through the application and operation of Biblical constructs.

LEADERSHIP APPLICATIONS FROM EZRA AND NEHEMIAH
- 2 Chronicles 36:22-23; Nehemiah 2:5-7
  - What is the mission of King Cyrus and of Nehemiah?
  - Write a mission statement for Nehemiah
- Ezra 1:1-2:70
  - Write a Master plan
  - List some of the team members of Ezra
  - Who are the stakeholders?
  - Who are the recipients of the mission?
- Ezra 3:1-3:10; 1:2-5; 3:7; 2:68-69
  - Identify the needed resources
  - Describe the commitment needed to accomplish the mission

The Blessing and Theology of Working

- **God blesses us through our working**
  - Proverbs 12:11 – He who forms his land will have plenty of food, but he who follows worthless pursuits has no sense.
  - Proverbs 12:24a – The hand of the hardworking will rule
- Having to work is not a curse
  - Genesis 3:17
    - The land was cursed
    - Work can be painful
    - Work is necessary to eat
  - Proverbs 24:27, 30-34
    - After work, the house is built
    - In Jewish tradition, after one is working, then there is marriage (Jacob)
    - Poverty is the result of lack of work
- Perceptions can be meaningless
  - Proverb 12:9 – Appearances are meaningless
    - We can pretend to be rich, while starving
    - It is better to be humble and work
      - May need patience to work at a job disliked for immediate blessings
      - Work up to a job of passion
  - Blessing to work with one's own hands

- - Better not to be dependent on another person
- Psalm 104:14-23 – Opportunity given for work is a blessing not punishment
  - God provides a cycle of opportunity
  - The benefits received negate pain of obtaining
- The theology of work provides for gaining skill.
- The theology provides for the use of the mind over physical strength. (Ecclesiastes 10:10)

Scriptural Reasons to Have A Career:

SCRIPTURES	GUIDES TO EMPLOYMENT & BUSINESS	BEING PREPARED FOR EMPLOYMENT	RESULTS OF MEANINGFUL EMPLOYMENT
Genesis 3:17	God's plan	Willing to work even in the midst of troubles and trials	Success over trouble and having sustenance until death
Proverbs 6:6-11	Do not be lazy	Have wisdom and perseverance	Supplies for the future, food for the present, lack of poverty
Daniel 1:3-5,11-21	Be of good service regardless of the community in which you live.	Obedience to God Wisdom Knowledge Education Training	Promotion, Status, Continued employment
Deuteronomy 28:43	Be in charge of the situation, and not the situation in charge of you	In obedience to God	You will not be the borrower, you will be the head, not the tail
Ecclesiastes 3:12	Gift from God	Rejoice	Food and Sustenance
1 Peter 2:18	Our conscience toward God	Serious responsibility	Commendations
1 Peter 3: 8-10	Our Relationship to Christ	To Be Courteous and respectful	God's blessings

Matthew 25: 15-30	Teaching of Christ	Investing and building on the talents given to us by God.	Prosperity and Responsibility
2 Thessalonians 3:8-12	The name of Jesus Christ that says do not be idle or be a busybody and not working	Diligently and appropriately using the authority to maintain order and quietness	Not to be a burden to anyone, and to have personal sustenance.
Proverbs 24:16		Perseverance	Success
Philippians 4:6; 4:13		Prayer, Perseverance	Success

God expects us to invest our life in work that expresses our talents and provides our needs.
- Mission – work that meets God's agenda on earth (reconciliation).
- It is not enough to do work that expresses talent.
- It is not enough to use talent for personal needs.
- Use talents to show God's love in our daily relations.

Jesus' work integrated word and deed, one was not above the other (I John 3:18)

Gifts of Grace and of The Spirit[3]

Romans 12:6-8	1 Corinthians 12:4-11	Ephesians 4:11	1 Peter 4:11
Prophecy	Wisdom	Apostles	Speaking
Service	Knowledge	Prophets	Service
Teaching	Faith	Evangelists	
Exhortation	Healing	Pastors/Teachers	
Liberality	Working Miracles		
Giving Aid	Prophecy		

---

[3] Richards, Lawrence O. Ph.D. *The Revell Bible Dictionary,* New Jersey: Fleming H. Revell Co., 1990, p. 943.

Acts of Mercy	Ability to distinguish Spirits		
	Various tongues		
	Interpretation of tongues		

Scripture Reference	Gifts for Ministry in Word	Gifts for Ministry in Deed
Roman 12:6-8	Prophecy Teaching	Service Showing mercy Giving (monetary) Encouragements Leadership
1 Corinthians 12:4-11, 28-30	Apostolic Proclamation Prophecy Discernment of Prophecy (of Spirits) Teaching Spiritual Wisdom Spiritual Knowledge Speaking in tongues Interpreting tongues	Faith Healing Miraculous powers Helping Administration
Ephesians 4:7-12	Apostolic Proclamation Prophecy "Pastoring" and/or teaching Evangelism	

REFERENCES

Bibles

Aland, Kurt, Black, Matthow, Martini, Carlo M. Metzger, Bruce M. and Wikgren, Allen (Editors) *The Greek New Testament* Munster: Deutsche Bibelqesellschaft united Bible Societies, 1994.

Barker, Kenneth, (Gen Ed.). *The NIV Study Bible,* Grand Rapids, MI: Zondervan Bible Publishers, 1985.

The Lockman Foundaton. Amplified Bible. Grand Rapids, MI: Zondervan, 1987.

Scofield, C.I. (Ed.). *The New Scofield Study Bible, New King James Version.* Thomas Nelson Publishers, 1989.

Thompson, Frank Charles, Ed. *The Thompson Chain – Reference Bible, New American Standard.* USA Kirkbride, Bible Co., Inc. 1983.

Bible Dictionary

Vine, W.E., Unger, Merrill F., White, Jr., Williams, Jr. *Vine's Complete Expository Dictionary of Old and New Testament Words.* Nashville, TN: Thomas Nelson Publishers, 1985.

Books

Adler, Ronald B. & Elmhurst, Jeanne Marquardt. *Communicating At Work.* McGraw Hill College, 1999.

Biehl, Bobb & Engstrom, Ted W. *Boardroom Confidence.* Questor Publishers, Inc. 1988.

Chewing, Richard C., Eby, John W. & Roels, Shirley J. *Business through The Eyes Of Faith.* San Francisco, CA: Christian College Coalition, Harper Collins, 1990.

Hackman, Michael Z. & Johnson, Craig E. *Leadership, A Communiction Perspective.* Waveland Press, Inc. 2000.

Moorhead, Gregory and Griffin, Ricky. *Organizational Behavior.* Boston, MA: Houghton Mifflin Co., 1990.

Munroe, Myles. *Becoming a Leader.* Puenma Life, 1993.

Richards, Lawrence O. *The Revell Bible Dictionary.* New Jersey: Fleming H. Revell Co., 1990.

Whetten, David A. and Cameron, Kim S. *Developing Management Skills.* (2nd Ed.). New York: Harper-Collins.

ABOUT THE AUTHOR

Brenda Simuel Jackson (BA, MA, Master of Divinity, Ph.D.), is a born again Christian, affiliated with the Baptist Faith. She is a member and Minister of New Prospect Missionary Baptist Church, and does ministry through BSJ Christian Seminars, a Prison/Jail Ministry, and an outreach and equipment ministry. She is a graduate of Wayne State University, and Michigan Theological Seminary. As a member of the Pulpit Ministry, she assists in the teaching, prison ministries and intercessory prayer ministry of New Prospect Baptist Church in Detroit, MI.

Dr. Jackson has over thirty years of experience in human services, education administration, and management, as well as part-time collegiate instruction. She is currently a part-time faculty member of Wayne County Community College District. She has presented at Conferences of the American Association of Christian Counselors, local church women's retreats, mission programs, Christian Education Institutes, State Correctional Facilities, as well as Professional and Community Programs.

Dr. Jackson is also a published writer who released her first book entitled, *A Journey of Redeeming Faith* in April of 2007. It is the first of four seminar compilations entitled, *Reflections on the Path to Wholeness*. The second of this series entitled, *Being Wonderfully Made,* is scheduled for release in September 2008. Dr. Jackson has also hosted a radio broadcast, "God's Teaching Moment." Her Christian Journey includes short term outreach mission assignments in Japan, South Africa, and Jamaica. Her goals include future short term missions.

A native Detroiter, Dr. Jackson is a widow, a mother, a grandmother, and the ninth child of Willie and Lucy Simuel (both deceased). Dr. Jackson is a called minister of the Gospel, and was endorsed for Chaplaincy clergy by the National Baptist Convention, USA, Inc. Home

Mission Board in June 2004. She is a certified teacher for the Sunday School Publishing Board. Dr. Jackson has been licensed as a minister of the gospel since November 13, 2005. Her vineyard is the prisons of the world.

BOOK ORDER FORM

Reflections on the Path to Wholeness: Vol 1
A Journey of Redeeming Faith
By Brenda S. Jackson, Ph.D.

Name _____

Address _____

City _____ State _____ Zip _____

Phone _____ Fax _____

Email _____

Quantity	
Price *(each)*	$9.99
Subtotal	
S & H *(each)*	$1.99
MI Tax 6%	
TOTAL	

METHOD OF PAYMENT:

☐ Check or Money Order (*Make payable to*: PriorityONE Publications)

☐ Visa ☐ Master Card ☐ American Express

Acct No. _____

Expiration Date (*mmyy*) _____

Signature _____

Mail your payment with this form to:
PriorityONE Publications
P. O. Box 725
Farmington, MI 48332
(800) 331-8841 – Toll Free
(313) 893-3359 – Southeast Michigan
URL: http://www.p1pubs.com
Email: info@p1pubs.com

BOOK ORDER FORM

Reflections on the Path to Wholeness: Vol 2
Being Wonderfully Made
By Brenda S. Jackson, Ph.D.

Name _____

Address _____

City _____ State _____ Zip _____

Phone _____ Fax _____

Email _____

Quantity		
Price *(each)*		$11.99
Subtotal		
S & H *(each)*		$1.99
MI Tax 6%		
TOTAL		

METHOD OF PAYMENT:

☐ Check or Money Order (*Make payable to*: **PriorityONE Publications**)

☐ Visa   ☐ Master Card   ☐ American Express

Acct No. _____

Expiration Date (*mmyy*) _____

Signature _____

Mail your payment with this form to:
PriorityONE Publications
P. O. Box 725
Farmington, MI 48332
(800) 331-8841 – Toll Free
(313) 893-3359 – Southeast Michigan
URL: http://www.p1pubs.com
Email: info@p1pubs.com

Notes

Notes

Notes

www.ingramcontent.com/pod-product-compliance
Lightning Source LLC
Chambersburg PA
CBHW052104070526
44584CB00017B/2332